SCHOLASTIC Phonics

Dinosaur Habitats

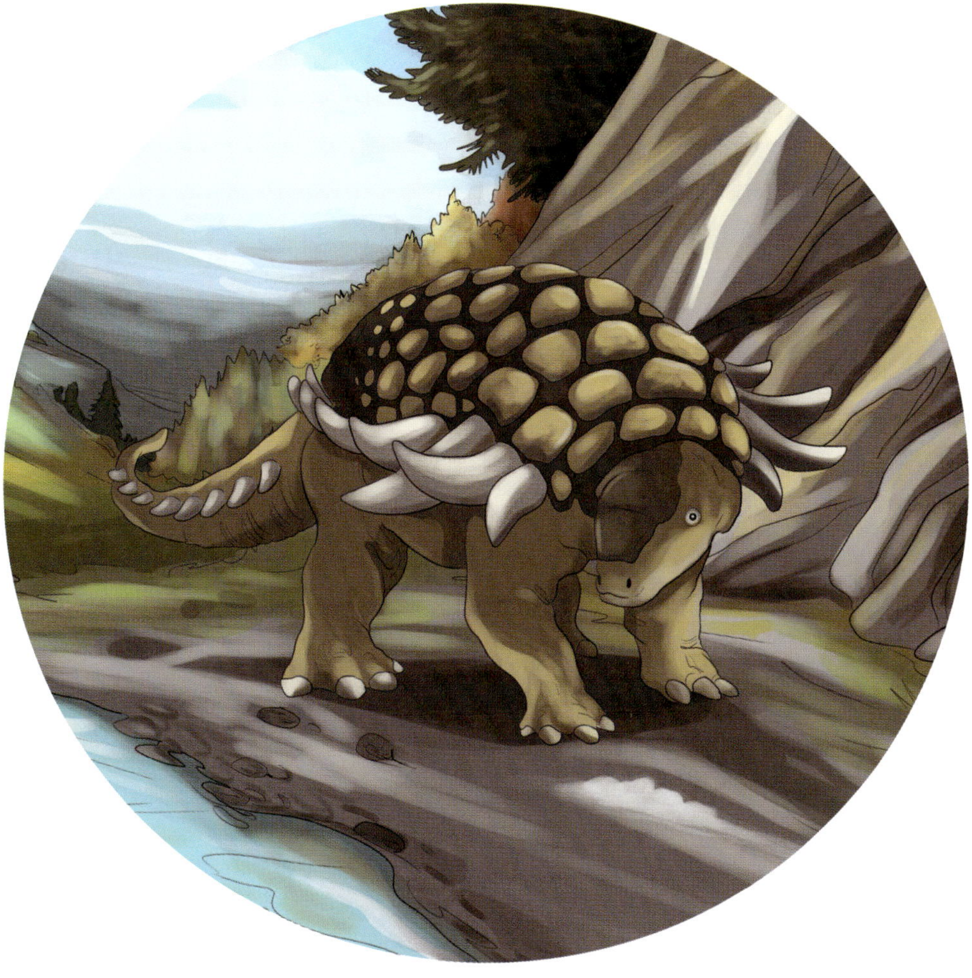

Published in the UK by Scholastic Education, 2023
Scholastic Distribution Centre, Bosworth Avenue, Tournament Fields, Warwick, CV34 6UQ

Scholastic Ireland, 89E Lagan Road, Dublin Industrial Estate, Glasnevin, Dublin, D11 HP5F

SCHOLASTIC and associated logos are trademarks and/or registered trademarks of Scholastic Inc.
www.scholastic.co.uk
© 2023 Scholastic
1 2 3 4 5 6 7 8 9   3 4 5 6 7 8 9 0 1 2

Printed by Ashford Colour Press
The book is made of materials from well-managed, FSC®-certified forests and other controlled sources.

A CIP catalogue record for this book is available from the British Library.
ISBN 978-0702-32116-0

All rights reserved. This book is sold subject to the condition that it shall not, by way of trade or otherwise, be lent, hired out or otherwise circulated in any form of binding or cover other than that in which it is published. No part of this publication may be reproduced, stored in a retrieval system, or transmitted in any form or by any other means (electronic, mechanical, photocopying, recording or otherwise) without prior written permission of Scholastic.

Every effort has been made to trace copyright holders for the works reproduced in this publication, and the publishers apologise for any inadvertent omissions.

Author
Alice Hemming

Editorial team
Rachel Morgan, Vicki Yates, Fiona Undrill, Jennie Clifford

Design team
Dipa Mistry, Andrea Lewis, We Are Grace

Illustrations
Ludovic Salle/Advocate Art
p5 (lightbulb) VectorCookies/iStock

Help your child to read!

This book practises these letters and letter sounds.
Point and say the sounds with your child:

- or (as in 'world')
- u (as in 'full')
- oul (as in 'would')
- aur (as in 'dinosaurs')
- a (as in 'plant')
- a (as in 'water')
- a (as in 'was')
- ear (as in 'Earth')
- sc (as in 'scientists')
- ze (as in 'freeze')
- unstressed vowel sound at the end of a word (as in 'Alaska' or 'polar')

Your child may need help to read these common tricky words:

many · the · they · were · of · who · sure · are · to · today · into · their

Before reading
- Look at the cover picture and read the title together. Read the back cover blurb to your child.
- Ask your child: *What is a habitat? Where do you think dinosaurs lived?*
- Talk about the image in the magnifying glass.

During reading
- If your child gets stuck on a word, remind them to sound it out and then blend the sounds to read the word: d-i-n-o-s-aur, dinosaur.
- If they are still stuck, show them how to read the word.
- Enjoy looking at the pictures together. Pause to talk about the information.

After reading
- Talk about the images on page 24. What can your child tell you about them?
- Ask your child: *Which dinosaurs appeared in the book?*
- Discuss which habitats your child prefers. Hot or cold? Dry or rainy?

Many years ago, when humans didn't exist, dinosaurs roamed the Earth.

They lived for a long time, all over the world and in different habitats.

💡 Habitat is a scientific word for an animal's home.

Many early dinosaurs lived by riversides.

Herrerasaurus would have hunted smaller, plant-eating dinosaurs by the shallow water and ferny riverbanks.

Other early dinosaurs lived in shrubland that was dry and hot in the summer, but not quite a desert.

Plateosaurus ate plants, had grasping hands, and walked on powerful back legs.

Diplodocus could reach the tall treetops.

Evergreen forests were full of pines and monkey-puzzle trees.

Much later, lots of different habitats that were full of life spread across the world.

Duck-billed Corythosaurus grazed on leaf-shedding trees and flowering plants.

Swamps and wetlands were hot and humid.

Spinosaurus would have roamed these habitats and eaten fish from the water.

Desert plains were open vistas with dry breezes blowing.

There wasn't a lot of food but the plains were perfect for speedy Oviraptors, who would have probably eaten shellfish and eggs.

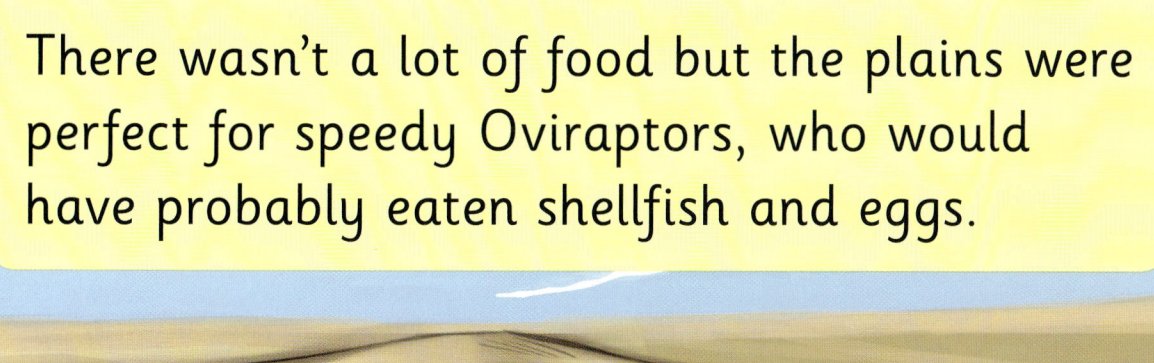

We are not sure if dinosaurs lived in mountains. Scientists think they probably did, but there are no fossils to confirm that.

Bones have been found at the bottom of mountains in Alberta, Canada.

Scientists have found bones in the polar habitat of Alaska. Alaska wasn't as cold then, but the ground probably did freeze.

Elsewhere, scientists have uncovered burrow-like structures. They think small dinosaurs squeezed into these burrows so they didn't freeze.

Scientists learn new things about dinosaurs and their habitats all the time.

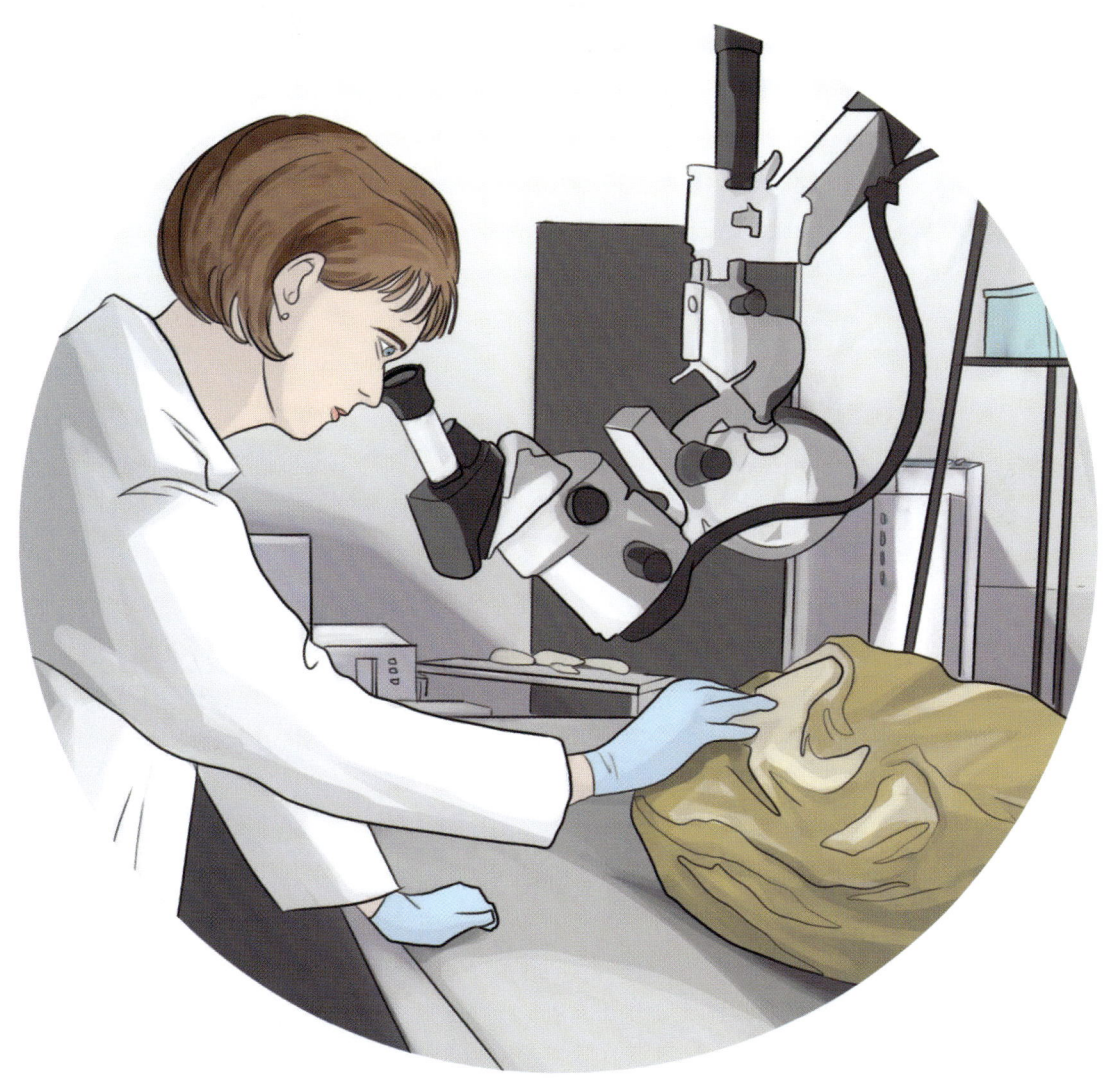

They work very carefully to uncover the fossils and study them.

Talk about it!